# GUIDE TO STUDY FOR SUCCESS

## An OMNI LEARNING CENTER Educational Guide

### LEARNING HOW TO MASTER THE MATERIAL LEADS TO SUCCESS AND LESS STRESS!

Study Plan

Mon | Tue | Wed | Thu | Fri

# MARGARET LOTZ

# GUIDE TO STUDY FOR SUCCESS
## An OMNI LEARNING CENTER Educational Guide

Copyright © 2019 Margaret Lotz

ISBN 978-1-950134-27-4
**OMNI LEARNING CENTER EDUCATIONAL GUIDES**
*an Imprint of PANGÆA PUBLISHING GROUP*

*Margaret Lotz cover photo by Marc Howard*

*Cover & interior design and typesetting by*
*DesignPeaks@gmail.com*

**DESIGN PEAKS®**

The book is available at special quantity discounts for bulk purchase.
For details, write to: *sales@OmniLearningCenter.org*

**Omni Learning Center**

25579 Carmel Knolls Drive, Carmel - CA, 93923
Telephone: 831-277-3387 / 831-224-0742
contact@OmniLearningCenter.org
www.OmniLearningCenter.org

This book is dedicated with love
to my students both past and present,
to my colleagues who listened and advised,
and to my family – John, Laura, Drew, Alexis and Torrey.

# ACKNOWLEDGMENTS

Special thanks are sent to Robert Ingersoll who set me on my path to education, to Dr. Lawrence deGraff who inspired my love of History, and to Lorraine, Hugo, and Connie, colleagues all in the pursuit of knowledge, with deepest appreciation and respect.

# TABLE OF CONTENTS

I. INTRODUCTION ........................................................... 7
    *TYPES OF HOMEWORK*........................................ *10*
    *SIMPLE STEPS LEAD TO SUCCESS!* ...................... *11*
    *DAILY STUDY SHEET* .......................................... *13*
    *WEEKLY STUDY TIME SCHEDULE* ........................ *14*

II. READING................................................................. 15
    *HOW TO STUDY A CHAPTER* ............................. *16*

III. STUDY AIDS – HOW TO MASTER A CHAPTER ............. 17
    *UNDERLINE* ....................................................... *17*
    *HOW TO USE POST-IT NOTES!* ......................... *19*
    *CHAPTER REVIEW*............................................. *20*
    *HOW TO DO A MIND MAP!*................................ *22*
    *MARGIN NOTES*................................................ *24*
    *HOW TO MAKE AN OUTLINE* ........................... *25*
    *HOW TO MAKE FLASHCARDS* ........................... *27*
    *COMPLETING A LONG TERM PROJECT*............... *29*
    *HOW TO STUDY FOR MATH* .............................. *30*

IV. PREPARING FOR A TEST – A MASTER STUDY SCHEDULE............................ 31

V. OTHER IMPORTANT TIPS ...................................... 32
    *AFTER A TEST*.................................................. *32*
    *WHAT SUCCESSFUL STUDENTS SAY…* ............... *33*
    *REMEMBER WHAT YOU HAVE LEARNED*............ *34*

VI. SIMPLE GRAMMAR RULES EVERYONE SHOULD KNOW ............. 35

VII. APPENDIX............................................................. 42
    *WORD CONCEPT MAP* ..................................... *43*
    *SEQUENCE CHAIN* ........................................... *44*
    *SATELLITES* ..................................................... *45*
    *DAILY STUDY SHEET* ........................................ *46*
    *WEEKLY STUDY TIME SCHEDULE* ....................... *47*
    *CHAPTER SUMMARY SHEET* .............................. *48*
    *CAUSE/EFFECT* ................................................ *49*
    *CALENDAR* ...................................................... *50*

# I. INTRODUCTION

Dear Student of all ages,

This is the book for you.

Learning HOW TO STUDY is the key to learning. This book fits perfectly with the maxim "*Give a man a fish and you feed him for a day; teach a man to fish and you feed him for a lifetime*." Learning how to study will change your life through the college years and beyond. You can take this Study Guide with you for high school, college, graduate school, and all future education.

Our society and therefore, our children, expect immediate results. They are told they are brilliant and gifted. So, what **IS IT** that happens as they begin to mature? Why doesn't learning come easily, quickly verifying that the child is a *genius*? The answer lies in how a student studies. The term "toddler" means just that…a young child is learning how to walk. The number of times they fall is without number, yet they *themselves* get back up, determined to continue on. The same can be said about riding the first bicycle and learning how to swim—the child would never stop, the challenge is too much fun!

The student wanting to master a class must take the same approach. They must take the approach of *"Fall down six times, get up seven!"* This is **NOT** an impossible task; it is actually enjoyable and rewarding if the student works in small segments and follows the steps within this book.

A typical student has **no work plan** unless taught. The initial evening may proceed like this:

1. Math / cell phone (this may be the class the student enjoys the most…)

2. History / Facebook, visit the refrigerator

3. Science / plays a game

4. English / internet, cell phone, email

The result...continual interruptions during study time and poorly completed assignments. There is no sense of accomplishment. Let's look at another student who completes assignments in a random order, something like this...

1. English / cell phone

2. Science / interruptions, refrigerator visit

3. Foreign Language (note that this is not on the original list...)

4. History / watch television

5. Math – the class the student dislikes the most.

## What reasons prove the Work List is WRONG?

1. You dread the evening. The other homework drags on as if the "Least Favorite Class" will go away.

2. Continual interruptions are wasted minutes

3. Too much time is spent on each class.

4. You feel that there is never enough time for anything else

5. Grades in the Least Favorite Class show no improvement

6. Most importantly, you feel under great stress. Why don't you understand the material? What am I doing wrong? Clearly, I'm not as smart as my parents say I am or as (insert any name here...) Everyone else seems to get it, why don't I? I must be a failure. I may as well give up!

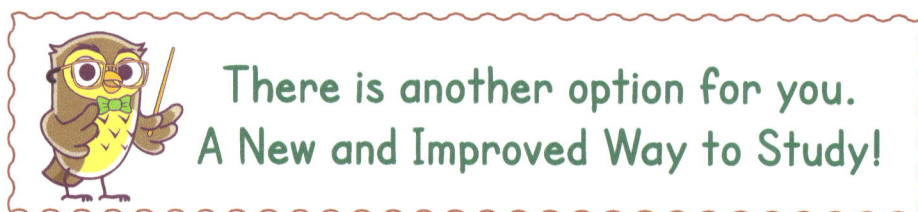

**There is another option for you.
A New and Improved Way to Study!**

Do **THE WORST FIRST**! Write Your Least Favorite Homework

Here:_____ (Write your true opinion. Note your teacher does not care. You are not "getting even here.") You write your **Least Favorite Class** to recognize this is the class that gives you trouble.

WHY SHOULD YOU DO THE WORST HOMEWORK FIRST?

1.  You have now completed what you did not want to do. You no longer dread tackling the remaining homework because the worst is finished!

2.  All other homework moves smoothly.

3.  You should find extra time at the end of the evening.

4.  Your confidence level goes up.

5.  And, your grades will begin to improve.

So, how should you get started? There are several steps so please follow them in order. Begin by emulating those who are successful. Business executives, world leaders, scientists, and others have developed a way **that works for them**. They may have individual systems, but there are overall similarities that are presented here. You will first make a schedule, then read or review, and finally you will make Study Aids. Study Aids that **you make** will lead to *Mastery, Success and Less Stress!*

## TYPES OF HOMEWORK

There are two types of homework. You are most familiar with the "doing type"…completing some type of short paper work, answering questions, or filling out a workbook page.

In reality, there is another type of homework which we call "Study Homework." **Study Homework means you Read the Chapter and Prepare for a Test.**

WHENEVER A TEACHER SAYS "READ PAGES …" THEY ARE ACTUALLY SAYING, "STUDY FOR A TEST!"

To improve your school performance and to give you more time after homework is complete (and therefore, less stress for you,)

**Follow the homework rules** in this guide,

**Do your least favorite homework first**, and

**Stick to the time periods**.

If you finish an assignment before the 30 minutes are up, then go on to the next homework. This means you "re-set your mental clock," **BUT DO NOT GO OVER THE SECOND TIME PERIOD OF 30 MINUTES**.

Use your schedule to plan your day and your calendar to plan your week!

😊 You will find wonderful improvement if you will be consistent with the recommendations in this guide!

## SIMPLE STEPS LEAD TO SUCCESS!        ORGANIZATION IS THE KEY!

### How to Study After School For Faster Work and Better Results

1. Begin your homework within 30 minutes of coming home.

    - Take a snack and change your clothes;
    - Organize all work on the floor, table or bed in the room you study; and
    - Put all papers, charts, binders, etc. out in the stacks you will use them.

2. Work in 30 minute intervals, or periods of time.

    - **NO INTERRUPTIONS OF ANY KIND ARE ALLOWED**. Discuss this with your family.
    - Set a clock for 30 minutes so you know when your time is up.
    - You must be determined to try your best. The main idea is not to rush, but to put in your best effort.

3. **DO YOUR LEAST FAVORITE HOMEWORK FIRST!**

4. You **must** stop working on a subject after this first 30 minute period and go on to the next subject. **STOP EVEN IF YOU ARE NOT FINISHED!**

5. After you have completed **two** homework time periods, take a break!

    - Dinner is the best break, but if your family eats later, then take a break of 30 minutes.

    IF dinner is later, then you cannot spend more than one hour eating dinner.

6. Return to homework after this break and complete 2-3 more classes. Remember to work in 30-20 minute time periods.

7. Some homework does not need (as a rule) a full 30 minutes. If you finish a class in less than 30 minutes, go on to the next subject right away. Keep working in the 30 minute time periods! By the end of the evening, **THERE WILL BE TIME LEFT OVER AND HERE IS WHERE YOU RETURN TO THE UNFINISHED HOMEWORK.**

**DO NOT RETURN TO ANY INCOMPLETE WORK UNTIL YOU FINISH ALL OF YOUR HOMEWORK.**

Some homework takes more than one day. **YOU KNOW WHAT IS DUE TOMORROW** so make a plan.

## DAILY STUDY SHEET

Learning to use a schedule can be difficult. Here is a sample Daily Study Sheet to get you going. The ideal situation is to use a Weekly Study Sheet so you can "see" your entire week. Both a "Daily" and a "Weekly" study sheet are here for your use. There are enough copies located at the end of this Guide to get you going. Make more copies when you need to do so.

Refer to the Rules for Study Periods on Page 10.

## DAILY STUDY SHEET

Time Started: _ _ _ _ _ _ _ _ _ _ _ _ _ _ _ _ _ _ _ _ _ _ _ _ _ _ _ _ _

Period 1 (*Least Favorite Homework*): _ _ _ _ _ _ _ _ _ _ _ _ _ _ _ _ _

30 minutes

Time Started: _ _ _ _ _ _ _ _ _ _ _ _ _ _ _ _ _ _ _ _ _ _ _ _ _ _ _ _ _

Period 2: _ _ _ _ _ _ _ _ _ _ _ _ _ _ _ _ _ _ _ _ _ _ _ _ _ _ _ _ _ _

30 minutes

### Take a Short Break (*Dinner, Family Chores, etc.*)

Time Started: _ _ _ _ _ _ _ _ _ _ _ _ _ _ _ _ _ _ _ _ _ _ _ _ _ _ _ _ _

Period 3: _ _ _ _ _ _ _ _ _ _ _ _ _ _ _ _ _ _ _ _ _ _ _ _ _ _ _ _ _ _

20 minutes

Time Started: _ _ _ _ _ _ _ _ _ _ _ _ _ _ _ _ _ _ _ _ _ _ _ _ _ _ _ _ _

Period 4: _ _ _ _ _ _ _ _ _ _ _ _ _ _ _ _ _ _ _ _ _ _ _ _ _ _ _ _ _ _

20 minutes

Time Started: _ _ _ _ _ _ _ _ _ _ _ _ _ _ _ _ _ _ _ _ _ _ _ _ _ _ _ _ _

Period 5: _ _ _ _ _ _ _ _ _ _ _ _ _ _ _ _ _ _ _ _ _ _ _ _ _ _ _ _ _ _

20 minutes

### RETURN TO ANY INCOMPLETE HOMEWORK!

## WEEKLY STUDY TIME SCHEDULE

Use this suggested schedule every day. It is designed to fit the rules for your Study Periods.

Write in the homework you will do. Remember to do your least favorite homework first!

After School Study Schedule:

### WEEKLY STUDY TIME SCHEDULE

| | Monday | Tuesday | Wednesday | Thrusday |
|---|---|---|---|---|
| **Period 1** <br> 30 minutes | | | | |
| **Period 2** <br> 30 minutes | | | | |
| *Take a Short Break* | | | | |
| **Period 3** <br> 20 minutes | | | | |
| **Period 4** <br> 20 minutes | | | | |
| **Period 5** <br> 20 minutes | | | | |
| *RETURN TO ANY INCOMPLETE HOMEWORK!* | | | | |

# II. READING

Everyone reads in a different way. This is a very important idea to remember. Do not compare yourself to a neighbor that you may think is much smarter than you. Secondly, speed does not mean comprehension. The way we read and interpret the symbols of reading are very complex, but for this guide, we suggest you keep in mind the following:

## Reading Aloud - Tools in your Book - Reasoning - Sequence

1. Reading aloud is actually TRIPLE learning. Your ears, brain, and mouth are working as one unit, and as an aside, all major actors memorize their lines by reading aloud.

2. **Use the tools found in your Book**. They are there for important reasons, and they are meant to be used.

   - Read the chapter **introduction** carefully. Read this more than once, especially the night before a test.
   - Many chapters have **questions** at the beginning. Test questions may come from this first page! These questions also make an excellent review for you as you prepare for a test.
   - Pay special attention to the **large bold print**.
   - Concentrate on chapter **sub-headings**.
   - Memorize the *italicized* or **bold print** vocabulary words. Vocabulary is **critical**.
   - **Questions at the end** of each section or chapter are good review tools.

3. **Reasoning** and reading go hand-in-hand. Use the vocabulary words and sequence to reason what happens in a chapter. Put simply, rain means wet, thirsty means dry, a puzzle means there are different pieces that have to fit together, etc. **Look for the sequence and apply your logic and reason to why events happen in a certain order.**

4. **Sequence** is a main tool in reading. The very simple words "doing things in order, usually by time," is often overlooked by students. All chapters start at the beginning and conclude with an ending. Practice asking yourself, "how did this begin? What happens in the middle? How does this chapter end?" These sequence tools will help you make sense of the chapter.

## HOW TO STUDY A CHAPTER

Read *ANY* Chapter by following these rules:

1.  Look at the title of the chapter. Repeat the title to yourself.

2.  Browse through the chapter, read the headings under each photo.

3.  *Read the first section of the chapter; read **just for the sake of reading**.

# DO NOT READ MORE THAN ONE SECTION AND DO NOT UNDERLINE!

4.  *Read the section a second time, underline important facts, dates or concepts. UNDERLINE the section, but **do not** underline too much. **Listen** carefully here…each paragraph has only 2 – 3 main points. **Look for, and only underline 2-3 main ideas**!

5.  Continue reading each section, follow up with the underlining for the second reading.

# The Important Thing to Remember: Stick to the Time Periods.

**Do not worry if you don't understand the chapter the first time you read it.**

**Work in small segments of reading.**

**Do you understand MORE after the second reading? If so, then you are doing your reading correctly!**

---

\*   Sections 3 and 4 may be the end of your first study day for a new chapter. You must stick to your time schedule. You will not have enough time to finish a chapter, nor should you. It may take you two nights, or more, to finish a chapter.

# III. STUDY AIDS – HOW TO MASTER A CHAPTER

## UNDERLINE

There are many pre-steps before you can underline.

1. Browse through the chapter first.

2. Read about 2 pages.

3. Using a pointer, refresh your memory. (Place the pointer in the middle of the paragraph and move it down at a rapid pace.)

Then…

Underline the 2-3 main ideas in each paragraph. It is very unusual to have more than 3 main ideas in each paragraph. Narrow the ideas down to only 3 if you can. Use ink or a highlighter. Do not use pencil.

1. Do not underline the entire sentence.

2. Be on guard for **bold** or *italicized* words as they will always be important.

Repeat the process with the remainder of the chapter in the time that you have left.

## Remember your time limit for each class.

1. Read 2-3 pages.

2. Underline 2-3 facts for each paragraph.

Reading is a very difficult task, and we should be aware of just how complex a skill reading truly is. Reading and mastery of the page are two different things. Underlining correctly is one of the most important learning skills that you can ever know. You can use these skills in underlining for any class. All books can be underlined, in fact.

IF you cannot underline in your textbook, you have other options:

1. Photo-copy the pages that you need. –OR-

2. Make post-it notes! (This is often a favorite skill of many students.)

## Examples of How to Underline

> ### NOTE:
> 1. Highlighting and underlining are considered to be the same.
> 2. DO NOT underline a complete sentence
> 3. A paragraph usually has 3 - 4 main points.
> 4. You only need to review your highlighting, NOT the entire page. 😊

### The **Battle of Long** Island is also known as the
### **Battle of Brooklyn** and the **Battle of Brooklyn Heights**.

The victory over the Americans gave the British control of strategically important city of New York. It was fought on August 27, 1776, and was the first major battle of in our struggle for independence to take place after the United States declared its independence on July 4, 1776. In troop deployment and combat, it was the largest battle of the entire war.

After defeating the British in the siege of Boston on March 17, 1776, commander-in-chief General George Washington brought the Continental Army to defend the port city of New York, located at the southern end of the island of Manhattan. Washington understood that the harbor of the city provided an excellent base for the British Royal Navy so he waited there for the British to attack. In July, the British under the command of General William Howe landed a few miles across the harbor from Manhattan on the sparsely-populated Staten Island, where they were reinforced by ships in Lower New York Bay during the next month and a half, bringing their total force to 32,000 troops. Washington knew the difficulty in holding the city with the British fleet in control of the entrance to the harbor at the Narrows, and he moved the bulk of his forces to Manhattan, believing that it would be the first target.

(Information taken from Wikipedia, *The Battle of Long Island*)

## HOW TO USE POST-IT NOTES!

1. Use 3" x 3" size Post-It Note (or larger)

2. Place 1 note on each page. Try to cover a picture or chart instead of any writing. IF the page is solid writing, place your post-it on another place while you write.

3. Write 3-5 important facts about this page. Be sure to use your own words!

4. Should you need another note...that's o.k., but try for no more than 2 post-it notes per page.

5. Do not let your post-it notes hang over the side of the page. Keep them neat and in order on each page.

You are **NOT** writing every single fact, every single event...**ONLY** the most important facts from this page.

**AND NOW FOR THE GOOD NEWS**...Once you have post-it notes for each page, **AND FOR THE ENTIRE CHAPTER**, carefully take them off the book pages, and reassemble them on 1-2 sheets of binder paper. You will then have your entire chapter condensed into 1-2 sheets of paper! Wow! Students find this study tool very helpful!

## Examples of Post-It Notes

### NOTE:

1. No complete sentences
2. Leave a space between each point
3. The goal is to shrink the information even more
4. Leave the post-it note on the page until the entire chapter is finished
5. 3"x 3" size post-it note is best. Color is your preference

• Washington successful in Boston

• Felt that New York Harbor next battle

• British arrived with 32,000 troops

• Long Island largest battle in Revolutionary War

• Washington knew he could not hold the city of New York

## CHAPTER REVIEW

### Almost ALL Chapters Look Like This:

Name of Chapter

1. Introduction

2. Section Headings (usually in large type)

3. Review Questions for the Section

4. Chapter Summary Review Questions

### How To Make a Chapter Review

1. Write the name of the Chapter

2. Make brief notes what is said in the introduction (skip if there is no introduction)

3. Write the headings of each section

4. Try to find 3 – 5 main ideas in each section.
   (There is space for you to add more information if you wish.)

   Turn the page for a sample Chapter Summary Sheet for you to do yourself. Again, there are extra blank pages for you located in the Appendix.

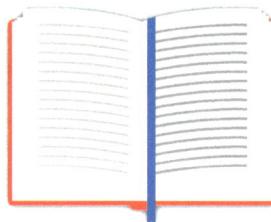

Example of a Chapter Review

## CHAPTER SUMMARY SHEET

Name of the Chapter

Chapter Headings

Vocabulary Words: Write the bold words on the lines below. Remember: <u>Not all</u> vocabulary words are in bold type. Be on the lookout for a treaty, special term, a person, etc.

## REMEMBER:

Trim the Information.                Find the most Important Ideas.
Use this form as a beginning. You may design your own form later on.

## HOW TO DO A MIND MAP!

### Please follow these directions:

1. 8 x 11 size paper. Put the title of the section at the top.

2. Make a Mind Map for each section.

**Then…**

3. Read the section carefully. You will need to read it at least 2 times.

4. Invent a drawing that summarizes what the section is about.

5. Put the other main ideas of the section, in picture form, around the center.

6. Vocabulary words are important in each chapter. List the words around the edge of the paper.

**Other Rules:**

7. No sentences, only words or phrases.

8. Stick figures, circles, "quick art" are perfectly acceptable. This is a "doodle."

9. Keep your paper neat and in good order.

10. Make your art as large as possible.

11. Use color. Color according to the meaning of the idea. For example, red is for violence, war. Green for peace. Yellow for new idea, alert, etc.

12. Stay current with your teacher's assignment. Do not get behind in making your Mind Maps as you will then have too much work to do.

13. Post your mind maps, in order, on the wall or the refrigerator. Refer to them often! Xerox copies if you wish to put in several locations.

14. Be sure to ask your teacher if you have any questions, or if you are having a difficult time finding an art idea.

## A Sample Mind Map

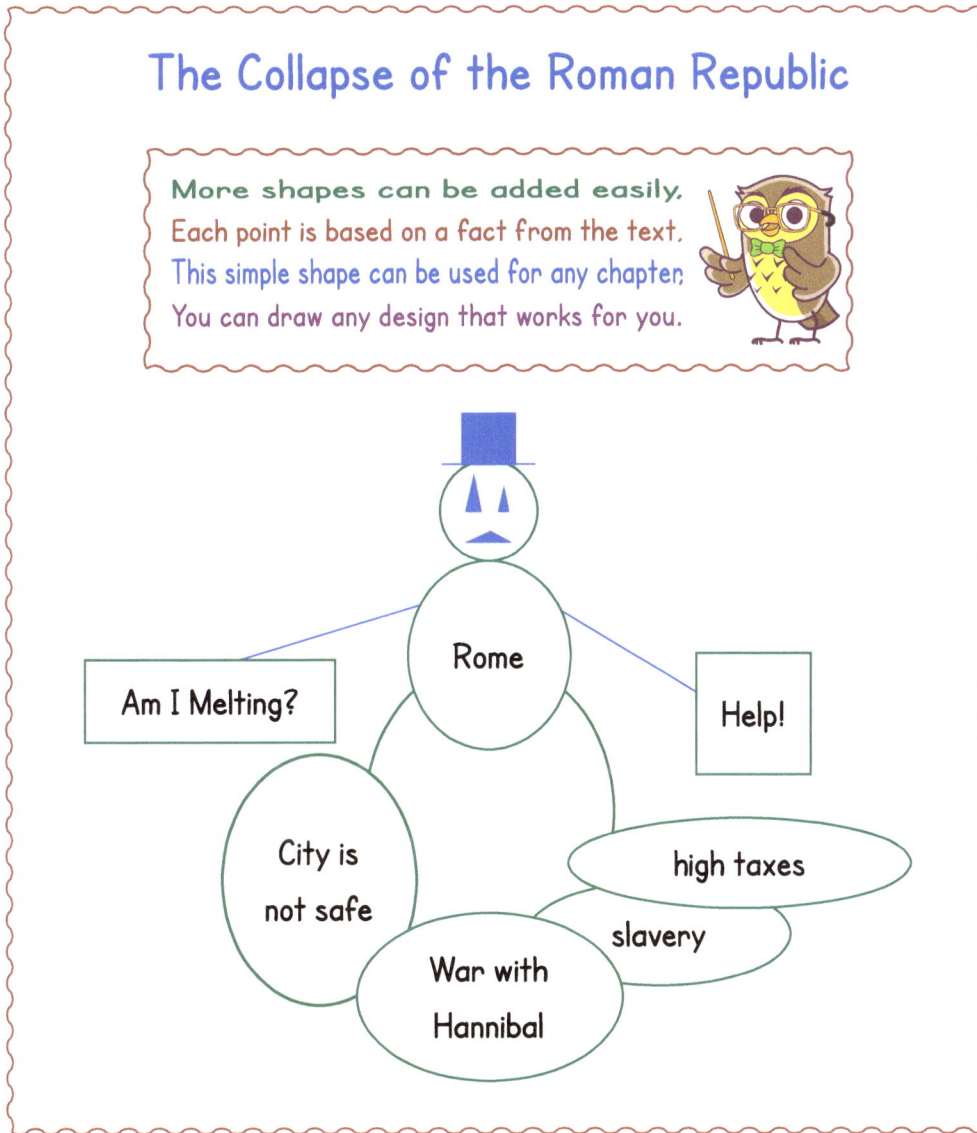

## The Collapse of the Roman Republic

More shapes can be added easily,
Each point is based on a fact from the text,
This simple shape can be used for any chapter,
You can draw any design that works for you.

Rome

Am I Melting?

Help!

City is not safe

high taxes

slavery

War with Hannibal

## Other Charts and Diagrams

You can find other ideas for summarizing your text material in the **Appendix**. You may like these charts better than making a Mind Map. The ideas remain the same—find the main idea and then use the sequence of events to complete the rest of the chart.

These charts include *Word Concept Map, Sequence Chain, Satellites,* and *Cause/Effect*. Keep these originals intact, but make a copy for your use.

## MARGIN NOTES

You have read the chapter, underlined all important parts, and the flashcards are finished. On approximately the Fourth Study Night, you are ready for a quick review of what you have learned.

1. Open your book to the chapter. What is important on page one?
   Are there bold print words? What are the main concepts on the page?

2. Write the key ideas in the margin of the text.
   Be careful here…do not write one word answers, write with abbreviated detail.

3. Make margin notes for each page of the chapter.

4. You should not need the entire 30 minute work time period. Work quickly! Go on to other homework. This is a quick review lesson to get you ready for a test.

## An Example of Margin Notes

### NOTE:
1. These are useful reminders of what is important.
2. Make Margin Notes after you have read and underlined a chapter.
3. Margin Notes are one of the last study tools to complete.

## Example #1

The Roman civilization began as an Italian settlement in the peninsula of Italy, dating | Italian penn |

| 8th C. | from the 8th century BC, which grew into the capital city and which gave its name to the

empire over which it ruled. A widespread civilization developed in the empire. The | Largest in ancient world |

Roman empire expanded to become one of the largest empires in the ancient world

though still ruled from the city. The population has been estimated from 50 to 90 million.

| A city-state |

## HOW TO MAKE AN OUTLINE

Outlines look like this:

**Topic**

  **A. Main Idea**

     a. Supporting Fact

     b. Supporting Fact

  **B. Main Idea**

     a. Supporting Fact

     b. Supporting Fact

        i. Additional detail

        ii. Additional detail

     c. Etc.

See an example of a complete outline on the following page

## An Example of a Completed Outline

### Collapse of the Roman Republic

1. **Farm land destroyed**
   a. food becomes scarce
   b. slaves work land
   c. farmers forced to move to Rome

2. **Rome becomes unstable**
   a. Not enough housing
   b. Fires and diseases very common
   c. No jobs in the city
   d. People sold their vote to politicians

3. **THE BIG problem**
   a. Poor hated the rich
   b. Rich hated and feared the poor
   c. Nation is not stable

An outline is **ONE OF THE MOST IMPORTANT THINGS YOU CAN DO TO MASTER MATERIAL**. Outlines do not have sentences; this is a quick "study" outline. Use the main ideas found in each paragraph and write what you think is important. Do you "see" how your outline is almost ALL of a section in your textbook? You have condensed 2-3 text pages into one outline! Good for you!

Note also that you can do your study work on your computer; just print out your outline. Flashcards can be printed, too, and you can leave the paper full-size if you wish. The point is to keep reviewing!

## HOW TO MAKE FLASHCARDS

Flashcards are very easy to make. Some students even think flashcards are fun to make! Follow these steps:

1.  Use 3 x 5" index cards or 5 x 7" if you prefer.

2.  Write the word and then write the definition. Note: Some people put the definition on the back of the card, but we do not recommend this as it wastes time flipping the paper to the back.

3.  Try to fit 2 to 3 words per card. Skip a line at each new word.

4.  Put all italicized or bold print words on a flashcard.

Other words for your flash cards are: people, **ALL VOCABULARY WORDS**, special events, or a word you don't know (wars, treaties, rules, people, etc.)

> **Do not assume that only the bold print words are important. Any chapter may have 10-15 flash card words, perhaps more.**

5.  Label each card with the class and the chapter. Example H, 15 would mean the cards are for History, Chapter 15.

6.  Keep your flash cards in a safe place. **DO NOT LEAVE THEM IN YOUR BOOK!** A sandwich bag works really well.

You will need these cards for the final exam and the cards are perfect for review. Store them in a safe place in your desk when the chapter and test are completed.

**Side Note:** Keep all of your tests, too. Check to make sure your score is correct. See your teacher with any question about your test or score. Store all of your things together. The tests made good review for final exams.

Example Flash Cards

> ## NOTE:
> 1. Perfect for locating an important fact
> 2. Perfect for easy memorizing
> 3. Perfect for condensing the chapter (to perhaps 8-10 cards)

Hannibal-general from Carthage, attacked Rome

Praetorian Guard-body guard of the Roman emperor

Julius Caesar-popular general fighting for leadership of the Senate. Murdered in 44 BC

Octavian-Caesar's adopted nephew, winner of the power struggle

Mark Antony-opposing general, defeated at Battle of Actium

Cleopatra - upon her death, Egypt became a colony of Rome

**We do not recommend 1 word per card.**
**We do not recommend a word on the front with definition on the back.**

## COMPLETING A LONG TERM PROJECT

The key here is to "chunk" every single part of the assignment, beginning with your CALENDAR!

Follow these steps:

1. **Mark the Due Date** on your calendar

2. Add any other important event to your calendar (other tests, major commitments)

3. **Read the Instructions carefully**. <u>Underline the important sections</u>.

4. Make a **rough outline** of the information needed for your assignment
   - Write an outline whether it is required or not. (Most teachers do require an outline.) *Why? – because the outline is the only way to guide your research.*
   - Be sure to get help from your teacher/librarian if you are unsure how to do this.

5. **Purchase supplies** that you need.
   - Index cards or binder paper
   - Cover for the final project
   - tell your family of the assignment. See Point #12 below.

6. **Be sure you understand** the types of material that you need.
   - Use only acceptable internet sites and books from your school library. Do not accept opinion as fact. Be aware of sources that may be suspect for quality research. **When in doubt, be sure to ask for help!**

7. **Work on the research paper as a regular homework assignment.**
   This means you automatically allow 20-30 minutes each week night.

8. **Write your research** notes just as you write you Study Flash Cards. Make sure you have a Bibliography Card as you must have a list of each source that you used. The bibliography page (Sources Cited) will be the last page of your project.

9. **Re-check the instructions**. This guarantees that you stay on track.

10. **Meet each deadline. Get help from your teacher if necessary!**

11. Take special care of this assignment as you do not want to lose any notes, instructions, etc.

12. **Print your paper at least 3 days in advance** of the due date. You print early in case there are technology problems. You also print early in case everyone needs to use the printer at the same time. Remember: *The Failure of Technology is Not an Acceptable Excuse.*

## HOW TO STUDY FOR MATH

Studying for MATH is the same
as studying for any other subject!

1. Make a list, or make flashcards, of important concepts, formulas and vocabulary. Math has specific terminology which you will need to know.

2. **Practice is most important**. Test yourself with independent practice. Check to see if you are right. **It is perfectly fine to go back to review a previous chapter.**

3. Break the problem apart. <u>Underline</u> important words in the problem and determine what they are asking you to do.

4. Substitute small numbers for larger numbers to simplify a problem.

5. Take a practice exam. Find some problems and treat them as a practice test. Give yourself time and don't use your notes or a book.

The more you practice math problems, the better.,
Math takes time and patience to master.
It may require more concentration than any other subject.

6. **Math is sequential:** Don't try to skip part of a math problem when you don't understand it. Instead, spend time trying to understand the process of solving the problem.

7. Know how to use the whole time allotted for the math test. Start out by answering all of the questions you can do more quickly. Check and redo doubtful questions.

Don't forget to ask your teacher for assistance.
Teachers love to help! 😊

# IV. PREPARING FOR A TEST – A MASTER STUDY SCHEDULE

So…here you are. You have completed the chapter and applied 2-3 study aids. We recommend reading aloud, underlining, post-it notes or flash cards as our favorite study aids. You have many options in this book –select the ones that you like.

> Test Day is now approaching.
> DO NOT HESITATE - begin to study!

You Need to Do the Following:

1.  Mark the test in your Calendar right away.

2.  Count the number of study days that you have.

3.  Make a Study Schedule! (Assuming you have 3 nights…)

4.  **FIRST NIGHT** – re-read the chapter underlines. Be careful, think logically, work on the chronology of events.

5.  **SECOND NIGHT** – Go over the Flashcards and all vocabulary words. Memorize as many as you can. Ask your family to review with you. Or, **READ THE VOCABULARY ALOUD**!

6.  **THIRD NIGHT** – review vocabulary immediately, and plan sample essay questions that you think are good. Before you go to bed, read the introduction and look at the chapter headings.

7.  **THE NIGHT BEFORE** – We recommend you look at the vocabulary one more time in the morning.

> Do not panic. Stay calm and reasoned;
> you have prepared. Good Luck!

# V. OTHER IMPORTANT TIPS

## AFTER A TEST

Regardless of your score…(but we hope you did well!)

1. Keep all materials! Be organized because you **will** need them again.

2. Make a file and store all notes, flashcards, and tests together.

3. If you are making computer notes/flashcards, make a file folder and empty all material into it.

4. Keep your test if it is returned to you. We recommend that you not share your results with anyone until you get home. It is no one's business what you earned on a paper; do not brag or boast about any score. We have all seen people who do that.

5. Many classes give final semester exams. The flashcards, margin notes, etc. will make it easy for you to review all of the material

6. Keep a record of your test score so that you can have a rough idea of your average grade.

7. **Do not hesitate to speak to your teacher** about any worries or concerns you may have after a test. It is their job to work with you!

## WHAT SUCCESSFUL STUDENTS SAY…

Will this new program work for me? What do other people say?

"Smart" students never think of discussing how they study with other people, but students who wish they had stronger grades think that these "smart" students are gifted, or genius, or perhaps have a photographic mind. The reality of the classroom is that there are very few geniuses walking around, but everyone does read and interpret material in different ways.

Students who have always achieved well and students that have made a major change in their habits (and grades) share with you what they do.

1.  I make sure I know all of the material on each page. I never leave a page until I am sure that "I have it."

2.  I try to tune in to key words that the teacher and/or the chapter uses.

3.  Just before a quiz or a test, I try to spend a few minutes reviewing each page.

4.  It takes me a while, but once I outline the chapter, I never forget it. I try to do a little bit of work on the outline every single day until it is finished.

5.  I find that re-writing the material is the best way for me to remember something.

6.  I read the chapter out loud. At first, I didn't like to do this, but it really works so now I do it all of the time.

## REMEMBER WHAT YOU HAVE LEARNED

Do you really want to fail? Yes…??? Then do the following:

1. Cram at the very last minute.
2. Blame the teacher.
3. Procrastinate!
4. Forget your books at school.
5. Refuse to work or review on the weekend.

You are far more competent and skilled than you think. This work is designed for you to succeed, but it does mean that you have to study correctly.

Remember that this book has tools you can use to *master the material*. To repeat, our favorite Study Aides are **READING ALOUD**, **UNDERLINING**, and making **FLASH-CARDS**.

You will have to read each chapter 3-4 times, or even more. Do whatever is necessary to increase your reading time. Read aloud because:

- you will remember each page in your mind,
- you will begin to memorize the material,
- you will feel good about your knowledge and skills!

Flash cards cement the vocabulary words in your mind. Each class you have relies on specific vocabulary; it simply has to be memorized.

Work in your specific study area, being sure to use the clock to control your study time. **DO NOT** allow yourself to be interrupted. *The goal is to finish your homework!* Work smart by using your time efficiently.

You **DO NOT** have to do all of the Study Aides in this book. Select the ones that you like. You will, however, have to do at least 3 (read aloud, underline, flashcards?) If these tools bring you success, good for you! Keep going. What if you fail the first time? So what? Begin again, but **ADD** another Study Aid, perhaps the outline or mind map. Keep going!

We **KNOW** you will see rapid improvement when you follow these steps. Never give up – it is hard to beat hard work! The ideas here have worked for generations of students! Good luck in all that you do!

# VI. SIMPLE GRAMMAR RULES EVERYONE SHOULD KNOW

## #1: There/Their/They're

- **"There"** means "in or at a place/point." *Think of there as the opposite of here*
    My house is over there.
- **"Their"** is *possessive*.
    We are going to their house for dinner.
- **"They're"** is a contraction of "they are."
    They're going to the park.

## #2: Its/It's

- **"Its"** is possessive.
    The car lost its wheel.
- **"It's"** is a contraction of "it is."
    Today it's very cloudy.

## #3: Your/You're

- **"Your"** is possessive
    Your pencil is on the floor.
- **"You're"** is a contraction of "you are."
    You're right!

## #4: Two/To/Too

- **"Two"** is a number.
    I have two apples.
- **"To"** denotes an action.
    I am going to the store.
- **"Too"** means "also."
    May I come with you too?

## #5: Who's/Whose

- **"Who's"** is a contraction of "who is" or "who has."
  **Who's** coming with me today?
- **"Whose"** is possessive.
  **Whose** shoes are these?

## #6: The Difference Between *Affect* and *Effect*

- **Effect** is a noun. (A noun is a person, place or thing)
  The special **effects** in the movie were amazing.
  The **effect** of hard work is success
- **Affect** is a verb – an action word
  Climate change **affects** everyone
  A lot of people have been **affected** by the floods

## #7: Well and Good

- **Good** is an *adjective*, which means it describes a noun
  He is a **good** boy.
  You did a **good** job
- **Well** is an *adverb*, which means it modifies a verb
  He is doing **well** in school
  The steak was **well** cooked
  I feel **well.**

## #8: Adverbs modify verbs

I run quick**ly**
He swims slow**ly**
The girls sings loud**ly**

## #9: Should've, could've, would've:

These words are contractions for "should have," "could have," and "would have," respectively
— *NOT* "should of," "could of," or "would of."

## #10: Than and Then

- **Than** is used when *comparing two things*
  He was faster **than** his co-workers at completing projects."
- **Then** denotes a *subsequent action or time*,
  **Then**, she put on her coat and went home."

## #11: Can and May

- **Can** means to be able to.
  **Can** you fix my bike?
- **May** is used when you want to ask for or give permission
  **May** I go with you?
  You **may** eat outside today.

## #12: Singular and Plural Nouns

*Singular means one*
*Plural means more than one*

- To form the plural of most nouns, add **s**
  **star - stars**
- If a word ends in <u>ch</u>, <u>sh</u>, <u>s</u>, <u>z</u>, or <u>x</u> add **es**
  **lunch – lunches; loss – losses; bush – bushes; mix – mixes**
- If a word ends in <u>ay</u>, <u>ey</u>, <u>oy</u>, <u>uy</u>, add **s**
  **bay – bays; key – keys: boy – boys; buy - buys**
- If a word ends in a consonant + y, change the y to i and add **es**
  **penny – pennies; lily – lilies; lady – ladies; bunny – bunnies**
- To form the plural of some nouns ending in one <u>f</u>, change the <u>f</u> to <u>v</u> and add **es**
  **calf – calves; leaf – leaves; loaf – loaves; dwarf – dwarves**

## #13: Possessive nouns

- To show possession, to a *singular* (one) noun, add apostrophe (') **+ s**
  Henry**'s** shoe
  Sarah**'s** pencils

- To show possession to a *plural* noun add **s** + apostrophe (')
    - The boy**s'** baseballs
    - The clown**s'** balloons
    - My sister**s'** room
- If a plural noun does not end in an s, add apostrophe (') + **s** at the end of the word.
    - The children**'s** sandbox
    - The mice**'s** box
    - The women**'s** office

## #14: Capitalization Rules:

- **Capitalize a person's name**
    - **O**liver **W**hite
- **Capitalize Initials**
    - **E.B.** White
- **Capitalize the pronoun I**
    - My friend and **I** are going to the movies.
- **Capitalize the days of the week**
    - **S**unday, **T**hursday
- **Capitalize holidays**
    - **P**resident's **D**ay
- **Capitalize the names of streets, roads, avenues, lanes, highways**
    - **P**arker **S**treet, **C**ardiff **R**oad, 10$^{th}$ **A**venue, **C**anada **L**ane, **L**incoln **H**ighway
- **Capitalize the name of a town or a city**
    - **S**an **J**ose, **M**iami
- **Capitalize the name of a state**
    - **C**alifornia
- **Capitalize the name of a country**
    - **F**rance**, S**outh **A**frica
- **Capitalize the name of a school or college**
    - **S**an **M**arino **C**ollege**, K**ensington **S**outh **S**chool
- **Capitalize the name of a business, store or restaurant**
    - **S**mall's **G**rocery **S**tore, **S**esame **R**estaurant, **A**lpha **B**uilding **C**ompany
- **Capitalize the name of a particular place**
    - **Y**ellowstone **N**ational **P**ark**, A**ngel **I**sland, **S**alton **S**ea

- **Capitalize the name of a language**
    **S**panish, **A**frikaans, **D**anish
- **Capitalize the first word in a direct quotation**
    Vivian asked, "**W**here is my book?"
- **Capitalize the first word in a greeting in a letter**
    **D**ear Fineas,
- **Capitalize the first word in the closing of a letter**
    **S**incerely yours,
- **Capitalize all the important words in a title**
    **T**he **C**at in the **H**at, **T**here's an **O**wl in the **S**hower

## #15: Periods

- Place a **period** at the end of a sentence.
    Abby broke her arm**.**
- Place a **period** after initials
    Ryland H**.** Gomez
- Place a **period** after an abbreviation for a day of the week
    Sunday – Sun, Monday – Mon. Tuesday – Tues.
    Wednesday – Wed. Thursday – Thurs. Friday – Fri. Saturday – Sat.
- Place a **period** after the end of each month
    January – Jan. February – Feb. March – Mar. April – Apr.
    August – Aug. September – Sept. October – Oct. November – Nov.
    December – Dec.

## #16: Commas

- **Place a comma between the day and year in a date.**
    June 27, 2007
- **Place a comma between the name of the day and the date.**
    Saturday**,** April 8, 2010
- **Place a comma between a town and a state**
    Carmel**,** California
- **Place a comma between a city and a country**
    Johannesburg**,** South Africa

- **In a street address, place a comma after the street and after the city.**
  19 Cardiff Road, Carmel, California
- **Place a comma after three or more items in a series.**
  The pet shop has lizards, frogs, fish, geckos, and rabbits.
- **Place a comma after the greeting of a friendly letter.**
  Dear Laura,
- **Place a comma after the closing of a friendly letter.**
  Your friend, Tori
- **Place a comma after a word like *yes* or *no* at the beginning of a sentence.**
  No, Drew did not come in.
- **If the name of a person is at the beginning of the sentence, place a comma after the person's name.**
  Alexis, when is your birthday?
- **If the name of the person is at the end of the sentence, place a comma before the person's name.**
  I like your writing, Vivian.
- **Place a comma when using direct quotations**
  "I love Star Wars," said Fineas.
  Oliver said, "I hope we have hamburgers."

## #17: Contractions

- **Use an apostrophe in a contraction to show where a letter or letters have been left out**

  | you are = **you're** | could not = **couldn't** | they have = **they've** |
  | what is = **what's** | I will = **I'll** | I am = **I'm** |

## #18: Underlining:

- **Underline the title of a book**
  <u>The Keeping Quilt</u> by Patricia Polacco is a beautiful book.
- **Underline the tile of a magazine**
  Students enjoy <u>Children's Weekly</u>.
- **Underline the tile of a newspaper.**
  <u>The New York Times</u> is a world-class newspaper.
- **Underline the title of a movie or a television show.**
  <u>The Princess Bride</u> was a delightful movie.

## #19: Quotation Marks.

- **Place quotation marks around a direct quotation. Be sure that the quotation mark is <u>outside</u> the comma or period.**
  Tristyn said, **"I love basketball."**
- **Place quotation marks around the title of a poem.**
  Kaelyn likes, **"The Land of Nod"**
- **Place quotation marks around the title of a song.**
  **"Come fly With Me"** is one of my favorite songs.

## #20: An example of a formal letter

123, 3rd Street
Monterey, CA 93904
June 17, 2019

ABC Construction Company
303 Mountain View Avenue
Anytown, CA 93906

Dear Mrs. Smith,

Thank you for the courtesy of our interview this morning. It was a pleasure to talk with you and learn about the ABC Construction Company. I am convinced that you will find my background and abilities suitable for the position of warehouse assistant. I look forward to hearing from you soon.

Sincerely,

Henry Smith

# VII. APPENDIX

We have included original copies of charts, graphs, chapter summary and a calendar that you can use to master a chapter. Be sure to work from a copy for your use, save the original.

The Learning Graphs may be used in a myriad of ways. For example, they are the best way to master vocabulary, follow the sequence of events, or to review for a test. We include here our favorites.

1. *Word Concept Map*

2. *Sequence Chain*

3. *Satellites*

4. *Daily Study Sheet*

5. *Weekly Study Time Schedule*

6. *Chapter Summary Sheet*

7. *Cause/Effect*

8. *Calendar*

# WORD CONCEPT MAP

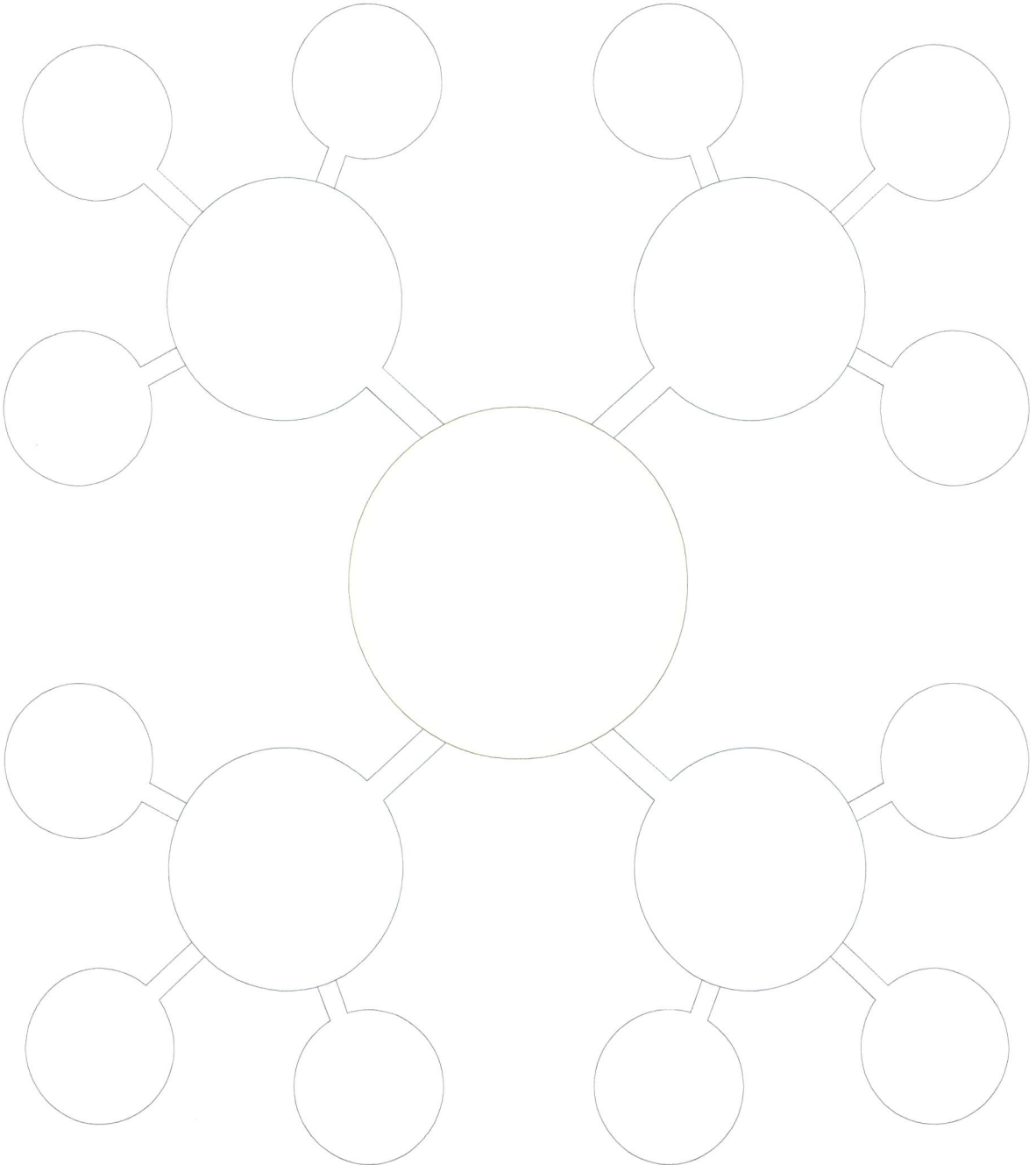

SEQUENCE CHAIN FOR _ _ _ _ _ _ _ _ _ _ _ _ _ _ _ _ _ _ _ _ _

# SATELLITES

## DAILY STUDY SHEET

Time Started: _ _ _ _ _ _ _ _ _ _ _ _ _ _ _ _ _ _ _ _ _ _ _ _ _ _ _ _ _ _ _ _

Period 1 (*Least Favorite Homework*): _ _ _ _ _ _ _ _ _ _ _ _ _ _ _ _ _ _ _ _ _ _

30 minutes

Time Started: _ _ _ _ _ _ _ _ _ _ _ _ _ _ _ _ _ _ _ _ _ _ _ _ _ _ _ _ _ _ _ _

Period 2: _ _ _ _ _ _ _ _ _ _ _ _ _ _ _ _ _ _ _ _ _ _ _ _ _ _ _ _ _ _ _ _ _ _

30 minutes

### Take a Short Break (*Dinner, Family Chores, etc.*)

Time Started: _ _ _ _ _ _ _ _ _ _ _ _ _ _ _ _ _ _ _ _ _ _ _ _ _ _ _ _ _ _ _ _

Period 3: _ _ _ _ _ _ _ _ _ _ _ _ _ _ _ _ _ _ _ _ _ _ _ _ _ _ _ _ _ _ _ _ _ _

20 minutes

Time Started: _ _ _ _ _ _ _ _ _ _ _ _ _ _ _ _ _ _ _ _ _ _ _ _ _ _ _ _ _ _ _ _

Period 4: _ _ _ _ _ _ _ _ _ _ _ _ _ _ _ _ _ _ _ _ _ _ _ _ _ _ _ _ _ _ _ _ _ _

20 minutes

Time Started: _ _ _ _ _ _ _ _ _ _ _ _ _ _ _ _ _ _ _ _ _ _ _ _ _ _ _ _ _ _ _ _

Period 5: _ _ _ _ _ _ _ _ _ _ _ _ _ _ _ _ _ _ _ _ _ _ _ _ _ _ _ _ _ _ _ _ _ _

20 minutes

### *RETURN TO ANY INCOMPLETE HOMEWORK!*

# WEEKLY STUDY TIME SCHEDULE

| | Monday | Tuesday | Wednesday | Thrusday |
|---|---|---|---|---|
| **Period 1** <br> 30 minutes | | | | |
| **Period 2** <br> 30 minutes | | | | |
| *Take a Short Break* | | | | |
| **Period 3** <br> 20 minutes | | | | |
| **Period 4** <br> 20 minutes | | | | |
| **Period 5** <br> 20 minutes | | | | |

*RETURN TO ANY INCOMPLETE HOMEWORK!*

# CHAPTER SUMMARY SHEET

Name of the Chapter

Chapter Headings

Vocabulary Words: Write the bold words on the lines below. Remember: Not all vocabulary words are in bold type. Be on the lookout for a treaty, special term, a person, etc.

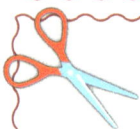

## REMEMBER:

Trim the Information.          Find the most Important Ideas.

Use this form as a beginning. You may design your own form later on.

# CAUSE / EFFECT

Name _____

Effects

Cause

# CALENDAR

Grade or Class _ _ _ _ _ _ _ _ _ _ _ _ _ _ _ _ _ _ _ _ _

Week beginning in _ _ / _ _ / _ _ _ _

| | Mon | Tue | Wed | Thu | Fri |
|---|---|---|---|---|---|
| | | | | | |
| | | | | | |
| | | | | | |
| | | | | | |
| | | | | | |
| | | | | | |
| | | | | | |

# OMNI Learning Center Educational Guides

## AVAILABLE NOW

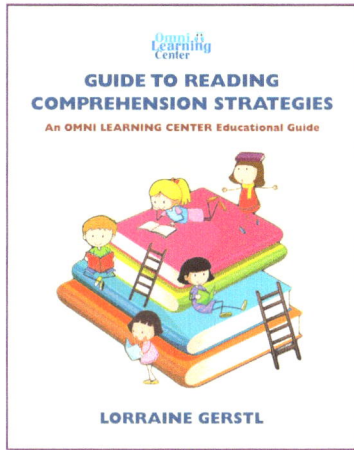

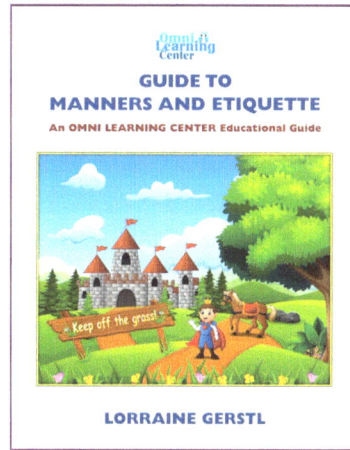

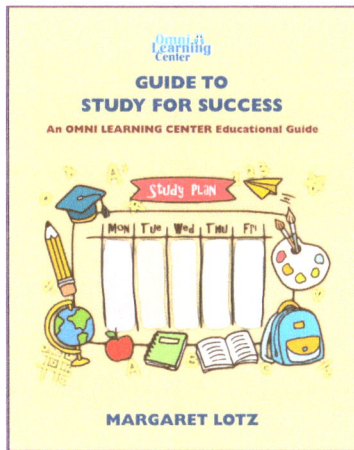

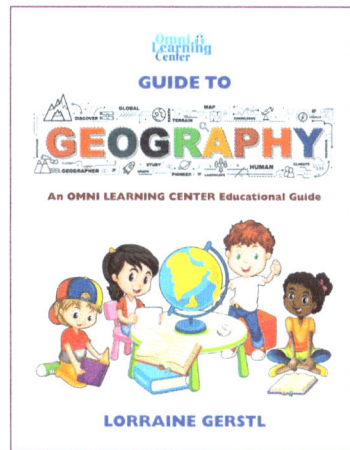

## Available Now!

**GUIDE TO READING COMPREHENSION STRATEGIES**
An OMNI LEARNING CENTER Educational Guide
**LORRAINE GERSTL**

**GUIDE TO MANNERS AND ETIQUETTE**
An OMNI LEARNING CENTER Educational Guide
**LORRAINE GERSTL**

**GUIDE TO STUDY FOR SUCCESS**
An OMNI LEARNING CENTER Educational Guide
**MARGARET LOTZ**

**GUIDE TO GEOGRAPHY**
An OMNI LEARNING CENTER Educational Guide
**LORRAINE GERSTL**

The books are available at special quantity discounts for bulk purchase.
For details, write to: *sales@OmniLearningCenter.org*

Omni Learning Center

25579 Carmel Knolls Drive, Carmel - CA, 93923
Telephone: 831-277-3387 / 831-224-0742
contact@OmniLearningCenter.org
www.OmniLearningCenter.org

www.ingramcontent.com/pod-product-compliance
Lightning Source LLC
Chambersburg PA
CBHW061354090426
42739CB00002B/25